בס"ד

קונטרס

אושר החיים

A Time
of Miracles

ימי נסים היו לישראל: פורים ופסח

(רש"י, תענית כט, א)

מחשבות מוסר

על פורים ופסח

נכתב בזכות הרבים ובסייעתא דשמיא

על ידי

אשר נחום סמיט

©All Rights Reserved

אדר א' תשפ"ב

Usher Smith

35 Kletsk Hill Rd.

Lakewood, Nj 08701

732-673-1089

אדר ופורים

The *Avodah* of *Simchas Adar*..8

Healing the Broken-hearted..11

A Purim Lesson – *Tzaddik Ve'tov Lo, Rasha Ve'ra Lo*..14

Mordechai's *Bitachon*...19

An Outcome of Purim - *Mishteh V'Simchah*.................22

פסח

Shabbos Hagadol – Going the Extra '*Parsa*': A Different Class of *Avodah*..26

Demonstrating Genuine *Avdus*..32

The *Seder* -- A Focus on One's 'Inner World'...............35

Ge'ula from the Internal and External *Yetzer Horah*...38

'*Hein Am Le'vadad*'..41

Pesach, Matzah and *Maror*..43

Acharon shel Pesach - Perfection of The Mind: Conquering the Enemy from Within...............................46

לזכות

מיכאל בן שלום

לע"נ

מרדכי מרקל

בן נפתלי הערץ

בס"ד

אפריון נמטייה לידידי הר"ר אשר נחום סמיט נ"י על הקונטרסים שמפיץ שמלאים דברים נעימים על דברי תורה שמעוררים ליבות קוראיהם ליראת שמים. ובזה ברכתי שלוחה שיזכה להמשיך לחזק את הרבים ויזכה ללמד וללמוד לאוי"ט מתוך בריאות גופא ונהורא מעליא עד כי יבא שלה במהרה בימינו.

אושר החיים Previous Haskoma to

בס"ד

בית מדרש
קהל אנשי ספרד
K'hal Anshei S'Fard * 13ᵗʰ St & Madison Ave * PO Box 693 * Lakewood, New Jersey 08701

הרב שמואל בלעך
Horav Shmuel Blech
Morah D'Asra

Previous Haskoma to אושר החיים

אדר ופורים

The Avodah of Simchas Adar

There is a disagreement in the *Gemara* (Megilla 6:) in a year which has two *Adars*. The question asked is, which *Adar* takes precedence in regards to *Purim*. According to Rabbi Eliezer b'Rebbi Yosi, *Purim* would primarily take place during the first *Adar*. While, according to Rabbi Shimon Ben Gamliel, it would be the second *Adar* -- the one closest to *Nissan*. The *gemara* then gives a reason for each opinion. Rabbi Eliezer b'Rebbi Yosi says that we should apply the dictum of *Chazal*, "*Ein ma'avirin al hamitzvos*". Therefore, if we would go through the first *Adar* without fulfilling the *mitzvos hayom* of *Purim*, we would essentially be "passing over" these *mitzvos*. Accordingly, it is better to keep *Purim* in the first *Adar*. However, Rabbi Shimon Ben Gamliel says it is better to wait until the second *Adar*, since *Purim* was considered a "*ge'ula*" for *Klal Yisroel*, and *Pesach* is a "*geula*". Therefore, it is considered of **greater importance** to bring these two *ge'ulos* near to each other.[1]

We may ask, what exactly did Rabbi Shimon Ben Gamliel see in the principle of "*mismach ge'ula le'ge'ula* -- bringing one redemption near to another", that it should be considered of greater importance than the *klal* of "*Ein ma'avirin al hamitzvos*"?

---

[1] מגילה ו עמוד ב: אמר רבי יוחנן: ושניהם מקרא אחד דרשו: בכל שנה ושנה. רבי אליעזר ברבי יוסי סבר: בכל שנה ושנה, מה כל שנה ושנה אדר הסמוך לשבט - אף כאן אדר הסמוך לשבט, ורבן שמעון בן גמליאל סבר: בכל שנה ושנה, מה כל שנה ושנה אדר הסמוך לניסן - אף כאן אדר הסמוך לניסן. בשלמא רבי אליעזר ברבי יוסי - מסתבר טעמא, דאין מעבירין על המצות, אלא רבן שמעון בן גמליאל מאי טעמא? - אמר רבי טבי: טעמא דרבי שמעון בן גמליאל מסמך גאולה לגאולה עדיף...

This may be answered upon understanding that which *Chazal* (Ta'anis 29a) state:

כשם שמשנכנס אב ממעטין בשמחה - כך משנכנס אדר מרבין בשמחה.

Upon entering the month of *Av*, one should begin to focus on the *aveilus* of the *Churban*. As the month continues to progress, this person's thoughts become stronger and stronger in his feelings for the loss of the *Bais Hamikdash*. *Chazal* are telling us, that the same holds true for the month of *Adar*. At the outset of the month, one should focus upon the miracle of *Purim*, and everything that is incorporated in this yom-tov. Upon reflecting on these matters, he will engender feelings of joy (see Alei Shur, Cheilek beis, Hahachana le'Purim, page 467). As the month continues, his *Simcha* will intensify by means of his constant *machshovos* about all that Hashem has done for us.

However, Rashi (Ta'anis, ibid., *divrei hamschil* "mishenichnas Adar") actually says that the reason to be excessive in joy, is because:

ימי נסים היו לישראל: **פורים ופסח**.

"these are days of miracles for [*Klal*] *Yisroel*, **Purim and Pesach**".

Thus, we see, that the thoughts of *simcha* should not end with *Purim*. Rather, it is an opportunity for us to take the happiness of the *neis* of *Purim* and **continue** the momentum after Purim, with thoughts of the *Nissim* of *Pesach*. Upon following these instructions of *Chazal*, we will surely be elevated to a higher level of appreciation of all that Hashem has done for us.

This may be the explanation as to the opinion of Raban Shimon ben Gamliel. It is certainly true, that passing over the *mitzvos* of Purim would, to some degree, diminish the significance that we attach to those specific *mitzvos*. Ideally, we should seize the first opportunity to fulfill them. However, an even greater importance than demonstrating our value for these *mitzvos*, would be to elevate *ourselves* to a much *higher* level, as this will change our entire future. If we can only bring our entire outlook to an even higher degree of serving Hashem, then this would be the most exalted achievement, and of the greatest importance.

Thus, by being "*mismach ge'ulah le'ge'ulah*", we allow ourselves to keep building upon our thoughts, while contemplating the *simcha* of one *neis* to the next. This means, that through these reflections, coupled together with the *mitzvos hayom* of Purim and Pesach, **we ourselves** will grow greater in our awareness of Hashem and what He does for us. This will in turn, effect how we serve Hashem and fulfill all of His *mitzvos* in the future. Therefore, this is our utmost priority, *even* if at the loss of passing over a particular *mitzvah*.

Healing the Broken-hearted

In the second Hallelukah that we say in Pesukei d'Zimrah each day, we praise Hashem as

הָרוֹפֵא לִשְׁבוּרֵי לֵב, וּמְחַבֵּשׁ לְעַצְּבוֹתָם –

who heals the broken-hearted, and bandages their sorrows.

The question may be asked: Isn't the posuk in the wrong order? First, it should make mention of Hashem bandaging the broken-hearted person's sorrows, and only afterwards that He will come to heal them.

Perhaps we can suggest that the posuk is discussing two distinct situations, and is therefore not giving us a sequence of events. The purpose of Hashem bringing suffering upon Bnei Yisroel is to cause us to do teshuvah - to bring us closer to Him. Therefore, Hashem can do this in one of two ways.

At times, Hashem will bring a tremendous fear upon an individual or the community without any actual physical suffering. The fear alone causes us to become broken of heart to the point that we come back to Hashem and His ways. Although nothing happened to us physically, this fright is enough to cause us to return to Hashem. Thus, at that point, Hashem will give us a healing from our broken heart.

This is what transpired during the unfolding nes of Purim. The gemara states in Maseches Megillah (14a):

אמר רבי אבא בר כהנא גדולה הסרת טבעת יותר מארבעים ושמונה נביאים ושבע נביאות שנתנבאו להן לישראל שכולן לא החזירום למוטב ואילו הסרת טבעת החזירתן למוטב -

Rabbi Aba bar Kahana says, "The removal of the ring [from Achashveirosh to Haman] had a greater positive effect than forty-eight prophets and seven prophetesses who prophesized for the Jews. They all did not succeed in causing them to repent, whereas the removal of the ring did cause them to repent."

The tremendous fear caused by Achashveirosh's transfer of his signet ring to Haman to sign the decree to annihilate us was enough to bring us back to Hashem. The fright itself brought us to teshuvah. Once this wave of teshuvah took place, Hashem orchestrated the miracle of Purim, reversing the Heavenly decree and thereby removing our despair. In that instance, Hashem was a רוֹפֵא לִשְׁבוּרֵי לֵב - He healed us from a state of being broken-hearted, without us actually suffering any physical harm.

However, there are other times that Hashem - with cheshbonos (calculations) that only He can understand - chooses to bring us back to Him through difficult and very corporeal types of adversities. Bnei Yisroel found themselves in such a climate during the oppression of the Yevanim, before the nes of Chanukah. At that time, we suffered physically. When we returned to Hashem then, He needed to physically heal us from our painful situation. This was וּמְחַבֵּשׁ לְעַצְּבוֹתָם - and He bandages their sorrows.

When we give thought to the miracle and salvation that Hashem performed for us on Purim, we must not forget that He did it in such a way that nothing happened to us physically. Hashem spared us from having to go through untold suffering, and instead chose to bring us back as שְׁבוּרֵי לֵב alone.

How often does it happen that one is not feeling well, has a pain of some sort, or some other symptom, and the doctor grows very concerned? X-rays are taken, blood tests are performed, and this person does not stop davening to Hashem throughout the entire ordeal! Finally, the doctor calls him up to tell him the news. "It's all clear. All the results came out OK!" Thus, Hashem was a רוֹפֵא לִשְׁבוּרֵי לֵב. He aroused this person to a state of teshuvah without any physical harm actually happening to him.

A Purim Lesson – Tzaddik Ve'tov Lo, Rasha Ve'ra Lo

In the beginning of the story of Purim, we find an interesting division between the design which Hashem has set up in this world, and *le'havdil*, the view of Achashveirosh. The commentary *Minchas Areiv* on Megillas Esther (1:6), quotes Rabbi Menachem Azarya, who tells us of how Achashveirosh had prepared the feast to which all of the *Yidden* were invited. He had set up an atmosphere in which those present would be surrounded with all sorts of pleasures; gratifications that would include almost all of their senses. The beautiful aromas of the roses and flowers from the Kings garden would tantalize their sense of smell. They were given the delight of seeing the most beautiful tapestries, such as *'chur karpas utecheiles...'* (1:6). Their ability to feel the comfortable couches on which they leaned, only added to their pleasure. Of course, they tasted from the most delightful foods and drinks.

However, there was one sense which was neglected. That was the sense of hearing, in which Achashveirosh did not allow any musical instruments to be played at all. Since, not every person is pleased with the same music. There are those who find pleasure in one type of instrument, while the next person will only enjoy a different one. As it would be impossible to please everyone, this would clearly not fit with the policy of Achashveirosh to do *'kirtzon ish ve'ish--* to give each one according to his desire'. Therefore, he completely did away with the idea of having music played by this party.

On the other hand, the *Midrash* (Midrash Esther 2:14) tells us, that although the plan of Achashveirosh by his feast, was, *"la'asos kirtzon ish ve'ish"*, Hashem had a different masterplan as to how to run the world. Hashem told Achashveirosh, "I do not give [in this world] what each one wants, while you **do** seek to give every person what they wish?! ...if there are two ships leaving from the shore -- one of them desires a northern wind, while the other wants a southern wind -- is it possible for one wind to simultaneously guide them both?! Rather, [it will be] either only for this person or for the next one. Tomorrow, there will be two people who will come before you, [whereas you will come to make] a verdict. That is, the *"ish Yehudi"* -- namely, Mordechai, and the *"ish tzar ve'oyeiv"* -- Haman. Will you be able to conciliate them both? Rather, you will elevate one and the other you will hang..."

We see then, a vast difference between the way in which Hashem directs this world, as opposed to the position of Achashveirosh which he had desired to infuse into his infamous *se'uda*. For, this view of Achashveirosh was clearly the antithesis of that which Hashem has planned for the world. Perhaps, we can explain that there is a deeper connotation to the approach of Achashveirosh, and a more profound meaning as to why he did not have Hashem's approval. Furthermore, we might try to gain a better understanding as to that which Hashem tells Achashveirosh about the dilemma between Mordechai and Haman. Since, as the *Midrash* above indicates, it surely contradicts the philosophy of Achashveirosh.

This may possibly be understood, by gaining insight as to how a *Rasha* looks at his situation in this world. For, the wicked live in a world of *dimyon* -- fantasy and imagination. They see their entire goal here, as being a life in which they can be ensconced in pleasure. Thus, to them, the purpose of this world is for nothing other than self-gratification. In light of this, we may be able to explain why Achashveirosh handled the affairs of his feast in the way that he did. As we know, Achashveirosh was a *chotei* -- a sinner, and a *mach'ti es horabim*. For, he sought to cause the multitudes of Klal Yisroel to sin by means of his *se'udah*. What was his end-purpose in this? His goal was to bring each one of Klal Yisroel to become completely ensconced in this world of fantasy -- to see that this world is nothing more than that of physical pleasure and materialistic enjoyment. If only he would be successful at that, they would completely forget about a life of *K'vod Shomayim* and bringing the *ge'ula*.

It was with this in mind, in which he instituted the philosophy of '*kirtzon ish ve'ish*'. If he could only indulge each *Yid* with every means of their own personal pleasure, then he would surely weaken them. This itself, was the very reason, that if there would be a situation in which he would wish to give each one their desire, but yet, it would cause someone **not** to get what he wanted, then he would hold back. Achashveirosh understood, that playing music at this great event would be desirable to many, but be unpleasurable to others. If so, he contended, then it would be a recipe for disaster according to his philosophy. It would certainly be a wakeup call for all those attending this party. Since, they would explicitly see, that while one might be having pleasure in this world, others will not. If life was truly meant for pleasure alone, then how was it possible that some were not being pleased?! Thus, they will be drawn out of the fantasy world that Achashveirosh had created for them, by internalizing this thought that there is more to life than merely fun and games. Therefore, Achashveirosh avoided such situations of conflict, in his outlook of giving each according to their desire. Thus, he felt it is better to avoid that pleasure completely, rather than give them opportunity to conceive this problem.

This is exactly what Hashem had told Achashveirosh in the above *Midrash*. Hashem specifically set up the world in such a way that one will benefit, while the next person will not. This is the lesson of *tzaddik ve'ra lo, rasha ve'tov lo*. Similarly, we find the opposite -- *rasha ve'ra lo, ve'tzaddik ve'tov lo*. This, explains Hashem to Achashveirosh, is the ultimate plan in this world. It is specifically set up in this fashion, in order that the *ovdei Hashem* will never forget that there is a much greater purpose here than a mere life of pleasure. Although this plan in the world will most certainly provoke us to ask questions (Berachos 7.), it will also demonstrate to us the importance of life. If the *tzaddik* has challenges, this may teach us that this world is only a preparation for a much greater place. Alternatively, if the *rasha* falls on hard times, this is to give us a clear picture of the vengeance of Hashem. Hashem continues to tell Achashveirosh in the *Midrash* above, that although Achashveirosh will try to bring Klal Yisroel to forget this true purpose of life, he will not be victorious. For, *sheker* will never prevail. In the end, Achashveirosh *himself* will be confronted with this predicament of *tzaddik ve'tov lo, rasha ve'ra lo* in the form of Mordechai and Haman. Thus, the fact that Achashveirosh himself would be the one to elevate Mordechai, while hanging Haman, would show that the truthful outlook will ultimately succeed.

The *Midrash* above continues with the words of Rav Huna in the name of Rav Binyomin Bar Levi. He says, that while Hashem had established the world in the above fashion, things will change during the ingathering of the exiles. Hashem will then bring a wind to the world that will satisfy **everyone's** needs." We might say, that at that point in time, the Glory of Hashem will clearly be seen by all and everyone will understand their ultimate purpose in this world. Therefore, there will be no reason for teaching the previous lesson to mankind. Thus, as the *Midrash* ends, *"Re'tzon yirei'av ya'aseh"*, Hashem will fulfill the desires of those who truly are aware of Him. This, is one of the lessons that may be learned from the miracle of Purim.[2]

---

[2] וז"ל המדרש (אסתר רבה פרשה ב סימן יד): לעשות כרצון איש ואיש, אמר לו הקדוש ברוך הוא אני איני יוצא מידי בריותי ואתה מבקש לעשות כרצון איש ואיש, בנוהג שבעולם שני בני אדם מבקשים לישא אשה אחת יכולה היא להנשא לשניהם אלא או לזה או לזה, וכן שתי ספינות שהיו עולות בלימן, אחת מבקשת רוח צפונית ואחת מבקשת רוח דרומית יכולה היא הרוח אחת להנהיג את שתיהן כאחת אלא או לזו או לזו, למחר שני בני אדם באים לפניך בדין איש יהודי ואיש צר ואויב יכול אתה לצאת ידי שניהם אלא שאתה מרומם לזה וצולב לזה, ר' הונא בשם ר' בנימין בר לוי אמר לפי שבעוה"ז בזמן שרוח צפונית מנשבת אין רוח דרומית מנשבת, ובזמן שרוח דרומית מנשבת אין רוח צפונית מנשבת, אבל לעתיד לבא בקיבוץ גליות אמר הקדוש ברוך הוא אני מביא רוח ארגסטיס לעולם ששתי רוחות משמשות בו הה"ד (ישעיה מ"ג) אומר לצפון תני ולתימן אל תכלאי הביאי בני מרחוק ובנותי מקצה הארץ, מי הוא זה שעושה רצון יראיו זה הקדוש ברוך הוא שכתוב בו (תהלים קמה) רצון יראיו יעשה ואת שועתם ישמע ויושיעם.

Mordechai's Bitachon

After Esther was taken to the *Bais Hamelech* under the watch of Haigai, it was to be determined whether she would be chosen as the new Queen for Achashveirosh. At that point, Mordechai went every day before the courtyard of the *Bais Hanashim*, to seek out the welfare of Esther; "*u'mah yei'ase bah*" (Esther 2:11) -- and what would become of her. Rashi quotes the Midrash as follows:

ומה יעשה בה - זה אחד משני צדיקים שניתן להם רמז ישועה דוד ומרדכי דוד שנאמר (שמואל א יז) גם את הארי גם הדוב הכה עבדך אמר לא בא לידי דבר זה אלא לסמוך עליו להלחם עם זה וכן מרדכי אמר לא אירע לצדקת זו שתתלקח למשכב ערל אלא שעתידה לקום להושיע לישראל לפיכך היה מחזר לדעת מה יהא בסופה:

"He [Mordechai] is one of two *tzaddikim* that were given a '*remez yeshu'a*', an indication to salvation. And they each paid heed [to it] -- Dovid and Mordechai. Dovid, as it states (*Shmuel Alef* 17:36) "*Gam es ha'ari, gam ha'dov hika avdecha*". [Dovid] said this matter [that I have such strength] did not come into my hands [for any other reason other than] to utilize it to fight... [and bring about a *yeshu'a* for Klal Yisroel]. So too, Mordechai -- it could not happen that this *tzadeikess* should be taken to be with a gentile, other than [for the reason] that she will arise at a future [time] to save Klal Yisroel. Therefore, he kept returning to know what would become of her in the end."

A powerful question may be asked on this Midrash. For, we can understand how Dovid saw that his ability to smite the bear and the lion was a '*remez l'yeshu'a*'. For what other purpose was he given this outstanding capacity, if not to bring about a salvation for Klal Yisroel? However, when we look at the story of Esther being taken for the purpose of being the wife of a gentile king, we would unanimously agree that this appeared as the greatest of tragedies. How then, did Mordechai see in this a '*remez*' for the salvation of Klal Yisroel?! Perhaps, we would be able to say that Mordechai had an unwavering *Bitachon* that all would turn out alright. But it would be taking this to an entirely new level to say that this was actually a '*remez*', an **insinuation** to the *yeshu'a* of Klal Yisroel?!

This may, however, be explained according to the words of Rabeinu Yona, in his sefer *Sha'arei Teshuvah*. He states there (*Sha'ar ha'Sheini, kapittel* 5):

ויש על הבוטח בשם להוחיל במעוף צוקתו, כי יהיה החושך סבת האורה, כמו שכתוב (מיכה ז, ח): "אל תשמחי אויבתי לי כי נפלתי קמתי כי אשב בחשך ה' אור לי ".

"One who trusts in Hashem should be hopeful, [even] from the midst of the darkness of his distress, for **the darkness will be the cause of the light [to follow]**…".

We learn from these *heilige* words, that *bitachon* is not merely as we normally see it. For, we would think to define the highest form of *bitachon* to mean, the ability to understand that although there is a presence of adversity, Hashem will make things turn out for the good. However, Mordechai *haTzaddik* was certainly on an entirely different level of *Bitachon*. He actually saw the difficult situation as the **cause** of the *yeshu'a*, as Rabeinu Yona stated above. With that being the case, just the same as Dovid saw a clear '*remez*' in his strength, Mordechai viewed the situation of Esther in no different of a light. To him, Esther's abduction to the *Bais Hamelech*, was a clear-cut indication, that a *yeshu'a* would come forth from it.

An Outcome of Purim - *Mishteh V'Simchah*

The *Rema* concludes the laws of Purim and the Orach Chaim section of Shulchan Aruch with a quote from *Mishlei* (15:15), וְטוֹב־לֵב מִשְׁתֶּה תָמִיד - *and the content of heart are always feasting*. The simple meaning of this seems to be that one should take the *simchah* he gained on *Purim* and continue with it all year long. If so, we can ask, why does the *posuk* use the word 'משתה' - '*feast*', instead of the word - 'שמחה' - '*joy*', which is more forthright ?

We also find that immediately after the *nes* of *Purim* took place, Chazal instituted ימי משתה ושמחה -*days of feasting and joy*. How can these two *avodos* of 'משתה ושמחה' be explained?

Acquiring *simchah* is not merely a good quality. It is essential for reaching *shleimus* (perfection) in one's *avodas Hashem*. Genuine *simchah* is a '*hergesh*' - a sensation that permeates every part of the person, including one's mind, feelings, and physical body. It can occur, for example, when one experiences something extraordinary, such as a *nes*. It can also occur while doing a mitzvah, known as '*simchah shel mitzvah*'. Of course, one may foster a more profound, constant level of *simcha*h by spending time to develop these thoughts.[3]

However, there is another method to upgrade one's state of genuine simchah. That method is to utilize **outside** influences to bring out the inherent *simchah* that is within oneself.

'משתה' is a feast of which the essential part of it is drinking wine.[4] Wine is a powerful means of persuading oneself towards *simchah*, as the *posuk* testifies (Mishlei 31:6), תְּנוּ שֵׁכָר לְאוֹבֵד וְיַיִן לְמָרֵי נָפֶשׁ – *Provide intoxicating beverages to the lost one, and wine to the bitter of heart.* Thus, 'משתה' is the act of persuading oneself to acquire greater levels of *simchah* through the consumption of wine [when done properly, of course]. For instance, the wine we drink on Purim brings out the *simchah* from the deep recesses within us.

We may now possibly explain the meaning of 'משתה' in the *posuk* above. We might say that wine is a *mashal* for the myriad kindnesses that Hashem endlessly confers upon us. Everything that we are given by Hashem may be considered the 'wine of persuasion'. An essential *avodah* in life is that we should be constantly persuaded to gain more and more appreciation of Hashem through the world of *chesed* He provides us. One can actually become 'intoxicated' from the

---

[3] Based on *Alei Shur, chelek beis, Hahachana l'Purim*.

[4] See *Targum Sheini* on the above posuk, as well as Rashi in Megillas Esther, 6:4.

myriad *chassadim* that Hashem constantly bestows upon him! Perhaps this is the *avodah* of the 'טוב לב' - *the content of heart*. He utilizes the kindnesses of this world as a vehicle to bring out the *simchah* from within himself!

Therefore, the posuk tells us, וְטוֹב־לֵב מִשְׁתֶּה תָמִיד. A person can become a *tov lev* – always in a state of happiness - by constantly utilizing Hashem's kindliness in this world to become 'intoxicated' with thanks to Hashem.

Thus, persuasion through the 'wine of life' is not merely a means of making one happier. Rather, it is the entire essence of the טוב לב. In other words, what is the quality of the 'טוב לב'? It is to be a 'משתה תמיד' – to always be persuaded by the 'wine' of this world![5]

---

[5] It is interesting to note that in the Megillah, the first two times that שמחה and משתה are mentioned as the *mitzvos hayom*, the order is 'משתה ושמחה'. In the subsequent posuk it states, 'שמחה ומשתה' - in the reverse. If one wants to understand the order of these *pesukim* in a way that seems to support what is being said here, see the commentary *Yosef Lekach*.

פסח

Shabbos Hagadol
Going the Extra 'Parsa'...
A Different Class of Avodah

The first time Bnei Yisroel fulfilled the mitzvah of *Korban Pesach* was right before they left Mitzrayim. The nature of the mitzvah during that first time was different than all subsequent times. It was done in three stages. First, on *Rosh Chodesh*, Hashem commanded them to take the sheep on the tenth day of Nissan. It was only after those ten days had passed that Bnei Yisroel actually took the sheep. Then, they had to wait another four days of *bikur* (checking) until the fourteenth of Nissan, to sacrifice the *korban*. And finally, on the fourteenth day of Nissan, they were allowed to sacrifice the korban. Why was this particular *Korban Pesach* so drawn out? Why was it necessary to wait ten full days until they were allowed to fulfill Hashem's command to take the *korban,* and then another four days to actually bring it? Perhaps we can find the answer in the following premise.

In the *haftorah* of *Shabbos Hagadol*, we read the *posuk* (*Malachi* 3:18):

- וְשַׁבְתֶּם וּרְאִיתֶם בֵּין צַדִּיק לְרָשָׁע בֵּין עֹבֵד אֱלֹקִים לַאֲשֶׁר לֹא עֲבָדוֹ

And you will return and see the difference between a tzaddik and a rasha, between one who serves Hashem and one who does not serve Him.

The posuk tells us that one can discern a difference between a *tzaddik* and a *rasha*; between an *oveid elokim* and one who is not. The *gemara* (*Chagigah* 9b) asks why the *posuk* categorizes two separate levels of serving Hashem - a *tzaddik* and an *oveid Elokim*? What is the difference between them?

The *gemara* answers that they are both considered *tzaddikim gemurim*, complete in their righteousness. Only, there is no comparison between the one who reviews his learning one hundred times – the *tzaddik gamur*, to the one who reviews one hundred and one times – the *oveid Elokim*.

The *gemara* then explains the difference in that one extra time of learning with an allegory. On the donkey drivers' market, they charge a *zuz* for taking a passenger ten *parsa*. However, if one wants to go eleven *parsos* – just one extra *parsa* – the price doubles to two *zuzim*.[6]

We learn two principles from this *mashal*. Firstly, while the average traveler only pays the lower 'going rate' for his trip, the one who goes just a bit past the 'normal' distance must

---

[6] וז"ל הגמרא (חגיגה ט עמוד ב): אמר ליה בר הי הי להלל: מאי דכתיב: ושבתם וראיתם בין צדיק לרשע בין עבד אלהים לאשר לא עבדו, היינו צדיק היינו עובד אלהים, היינו רשע היינו אשר לא עבדו! - אמר ליה: עבדו ולא עבדו - תרוייהו צדיקי גמורי נינהו. ואינו דומה שונה פרקו מאה פעמים לשונה פרקו מאה ואחד. - אמר ליה: ומשום חד זימנא קרי ליה לא עבדו? אמר ליה: אין, צא ולמד משוק של חמרין: עשרה פרסי - בזוזא, חד עשר פרסי - בתרי זוזי.

pay double! Who would be willing to pay such an exorbitant sum? Certainly, only someone who has a **strong will** and **desire** to get to that further distance, for whatever reason it may be.

The *mashal* also teaches us another point. The same donkey that took the traveler the first ten *parsa*, also takes him the extra, additional *parsa* (see Rashi).[7] To continue the extra *parsa* is not such a big deal. However, it transforms the regular 'ten *parsa* donkey' into an 'eleven *parsa* donkey', making it considerably more valuable.

This is the difference between a *tzaddik gamur* and the higher *madreigah* (level) of an *oveid elokim*. The *tzaddik* is someone who does everything he is meant to do, to the detail. However, he does everything within the realm of what is regular practice. He does what everyone is expected to strive towards.

The *oveid elokim* also does everything that is expected of him, of course. However, in addition, he is constantly looking to further his service of Hashem – to go the 'extra *parsa*'. Why is this so? Because of his **strong will** and burning **desire** to serve Hashem even beyond what is expected. He is always looking for ways to enhance his *avodas Hashem*, even if just a little bit.

Truthfully, the 'little extra' that the *oveid elokim* takes upon himself might not be that much more. Yet, his mindset to

---

[7] רש"י שם, ד"ה עשרה פרסי, וז"ל: עשרה פרסי, ישכיר לך אדם חמורו בזוז אחד, שכבר נהגו כן, ואם תאמר לו לילך פרסה יותר - ישאלך שני זוזים.

do a little extra transforms the quality of his first one hundred times too. It transforms his **entire** *avodah* into a new realm of being an '*oveid elokim*'. His *eichus*, his quality of *avodas Hashem*, enters a different class than everyone else's. It shows that even when he serves Hashem in the regular matters, it is not merely in the capacity of a '*tzaddik gamur*', but rather in the capacity of an '*oveid elokim*'– one whose strong desire to be *oveid Hashem* causes him to go above the norm, in his way of thinking, as well as in his actions.

When the *mashgiach* of Yeshivas Ponovez, Rav Yechezkel Levenstein zt"l, was by the *levaya* of the Brisker Rav zt"l, he was accompanied by another person. After the *levaya*, it was getting late, and everyone needed to *daven Minchah* by the Central Bus Station. While the assembled were about to begin, the person accompanying Rav Chatzkel noticed that he took out an orange and began eating it. Rav Chatzkel explained to his perplexed attendant that he wanted to make the proper *hachanos* (preparations) for *tefillah*. Apparently, earlier in the day, he understood that he may have to *daven* 'on the road' after the *levaya*. He also realized that he may not have the proper energy to concentrate on *davening* properly in such a setting. So, he prepared this orange to eat, to restore his strength before *davening*![8] Such is the approach of a true '*oveid elokim*'. Rav Chatzkel had the foresight to do a little "extra" to make a proper *hachanah* for *davening*. This surely elevated his

---

[8] *Sefer L'sitcha Elyon, Parshas Tzav*.

overall level of a *'mispallel'* above others who did not do the little bit extra.

This is possibly the reason the Korban Pesach was spread out over such a long period of time.

Although they were commanded to do this mitzvah by Hashem, it was surely not easy for them. Being that the sheep were the *avodah zarah* of Mitzrayim, it was uncomfortable at best, and fearful at worst, for the Bnei Yisroel to take the sheep as their *korban*. Therefore, they were given the mitzvah of taking the *korban* ten days before actually doing it. This prolonged time could have resulted in a decline of their initial excitement for the mitzvah. They could have entertained within themselves the possibility of not going ahead with the mitzvah. Of course, in the end they would fulfill Hashem's command. But what would their thoughts be in the interim?

During the four days of *bikur,* these doubts could have grown even stronger. At that point, they had the sheep in their possession already. It was very real and tangible. They could have easily began having second thoughts now. Maybe they shouldn't take the next step of actually sacrificing the animals? Slaughtering the sheep would surely upset the Mitzriyim! Once again, the actual mitzvah would undoubtedly be fulfilled. But what would they be thinking during the days that led up to it?

The Bnei Yisroel clearly needed merits to leave Mitzrayim. Therefore, Hashem gave them this mitzvah of bringing the

Korban Pesach.[9] However, He did not merely give them the actual mitzvah. He deliberately gave it to them in the form of transforming them into *'ovdei elokim'*, thereby making it a much greater *zechus*. How did He do this?

Hashem knew that Bnei Yisroel would not merely fulfill this mitzvah properly, as they were commanded. He knew that they would have a **strong will** and **desire** to go ahead with the mitzvah. Therefore, He commanded them ten days in advance, and they spent those days waiting in great anticipation and excitement to fulfill the mitzvah! True, they couldn't actually fulfill the taking of the *korban* at the time it was commanded. However, their acceptance of the mitzvah with such feelings of enthusiasm made it as if they actually already fulfilled it![10]

Similarly, the command of the four days of *bikur* was carried out with great alacrity, with a strong will to fulfill the *r'tzon Hashem*.

It was this extra time before the actual carrying out of the mitzvah that was the means of showing their status of being *'ovdei elokim'*. Most certainly then, the actual fulfillment of the mitzvah itself was done with this same measure.

---

[9] See Rashi, Shemos, 12:6.
[10] See Rashi, Shemos 12:28, quoting the *Mechilta*.

Demonstrating Genuine *Avdus*

On *Erev Pesach*, we adhere to the rule of not eating too much from after a specific time up until dark (see Mishna, Pesachim 99:). The Rashbam explains, "So that one should eat the *Matzah* of *Mitzvah* with an appetite, as an **enhancement of the *Mitzvah*** (*'hiddur Mitzvah'*)".[11] [12] The question arises, we may understand that there is a concept of making a 'fence' for a *Mitzvah* so as not to come to **transgress** that *Mitzvah*. However, we must understand the words of the Rashbam who tells us a seemingly more novel concept. How can it be explained that *Chazal* made a *geder* for a **hiddur** mitzvah? Since, **enhancing** and **beautifying** the *Mitzvah* is all relative to the person who seeks to fulfill it. It all depends on his inner feelings of *ahavas Hashem*, and a longing for the *Mitzvah*. If one feels that he is able to beautify the *Mitzvah*, then of course he is encouraged to do so. However, would we say that *Chazal* would go so far as to set a **boundary**, so as to ensure that the *Mitzvah* is done with *hiddur*? After all, enhancing a *Mitzvah* is considered **above** the level of a standard *Mitzvah*?

Perhaps, we can say that the night of the *seder* which represents the time that we are *yotz'ei le'cheirus*, is when we take upon ourselves to be the faithful servants of

---

[11] רשב"ם פסחים צט, ב: לא יאכל אדם כו'. כדי שיאכל מצה של מצוה לתיאבון משום הידור מצוה:

[12] See the Ran, who disagrees and learns that by eating on *Erev Pesach*, this might bring him to '*achila gasa*' when eating the *matza*. Accordingly, this would not be considered a form of proper eating, and is considered as though he did not fulfill the *Mitzvah* of eating *matzah* at all. See Reshash.

Hashem. Thus, it is at this moment - when we fulfill the *Mitzvos* of the *seder*, in which we may contemplate **how** to complete them. Surely, we may carefully swallow down the *shiurim* of *matzos* and wine, ensuring that the Mitzvos are done correctly. However, are they just 'dry' *Mitzvos* in which we are merely fulfilling them out of '*frumkeit*'? Or will we actually incorporate thoughts of authentic *ahavah* for Hashem and His *Mitzvos* while carrying them out? This night is the time that we take upon ourselves **true** *avdus* to Hashem. Most certainly then, Hashem wants us to be *leibidige ovdei Hashem*, rather than to merely fulfill the *Mitzvos* in a cut and dry fashion.

Thus, it is specifically on this night, in which the '*hiddur*' *mitzvah* of eating the *matzah* with an appetite is especially important. For, when we take pleasure in the *matzoh* rather than merely mechanically fulfilling the *Mitzvah*, this will allow us to express an even greater appreciation and alacrity towards Hashem.

It follows then, that there are two parts to the *avodah* of eating *matzoh*. Most definitely, we are meant to be meticulous in the actual fulfillment of the *Mitzvah*. However, more than that alone, is the ability to derive a pleasure for the *Mitzvah* which Hashem has given us. We are meant to appreciate every bite of the *matzah*, as we continue to chew it.

Similarly, in *Parshas* Vayikra we find how the *Cohen* eats from the *Korban Mincha*. Rav Avigdor Miller *zt"l* writes upon this subject (A Kingdom of Cohanim, in *Parshas Tzav* 6:19), that "the physical pleasure of ingesting the sacred offering is compared to the fire on the *Mizbeach*...The fact that we, "the nation of *Cohanim*" (Shmos 19:6) eat *Matzah* on Pesach night with appetite is not a blemish in our *Mitzvah*; on the contrary, we are admonished to refrain from much food in the day, in order to eat the *Matzah* with more appetite (Pesachim 99:), "because it is an honor for the *Mitzvah*" (Rashi)…"

Therefore, we see that the '*hiddur*', the enhancement of the *Mitzvah*, is the hallmark of a sincere *oveid Hashem*. This is an especially significant point to carry out on the night of the *seder*, as this is the time in which we celebrate our freedom, giving us the ability to become genuine servants of Hashem. Therefore, *Chazal* saw fit to actually make a 'boundary', demonstrating the importance of fulfilling the *Mitzvos* of this night with eagerness.

The *Seder* -- A Focus on One's 'Inner World'

הא לחמא עניא די אכלו אבהתנא בארעא דמצרים.
כל דכפין ייתי וייכול

The *Haggadah* begins with the statement, "*Ha lachma anya...*", "This is the 'poor man's bread' which our fathers ate in *Mitzrayim...*". We may ask two integral questions on this phrase. First, why is it that we begin the *seder* with these specific words; what is especially significant about this statement? Secondly, we might wonder as to the particular relevance of the next few words, "כל דכפין ייתי וייכול". What is the connection, if any, between these two subjects mentioned in this phrase? How does the poor-man's bread that we ate in *Mitzrayim* correlate with that which we invite the destitute to come partake in our meal?

Rav Shlomo Wolbe *zt"l* (Alei Shur, *Cheilek Rishon*, *P'sicha la'avodah pratis*) tells us of the 'inner world' that we all inherently possess and the importance of connecting to it. Most people live their lives with a focus upon the world that is around them rather than delving within themselves, into their innermost world. How is it possible for one to live with a focus towards himself in a positive way?

Rav Wolbe quotes in the name of the Ba'al Shem Tov *zt"l*, that everything which we look at from the world around us is like a mirror in which the *hashgocha ha'elyona* is showing us a picture of ourselves. In other words, all of the behaviors and actions of others should be viewed as though we ourselves are in that situation. This is what is meant by focusing inwardly upon oneself.

Chazal tell us, for example, that one who sees a *Sotah* in her state of destruction, should remove any association of wine from himself (Sotah 2:). This is so, because when one sees a person in a state of ruin, he should not merely look down in dismay upon that person. Rather, he should look inwardly, by telling himself of the danger that could face him as well unless he makes a means to protect himself. Surely, it would be more beneficial to find strategies to avoid causing himself to stumble in this same iniquity, instead of allowing himself to be angered over the actions of another.

The same would hold true in a positive sense. If he sees constructive conducts that are done by others, the 'inner-self' approach would be to arouse himself with a longing towards doing these *hanhagos*.

Perhaps, this is why *Chazal* decided to begin the *Haggadah* with the words "*Ha lachma anya*" followed by the statement of "*kol dichfin yeisei viyeichol*". This is stating, that in *Mitzrayim* we were treated in the most difficult way possible. Treated like simple slaves, we were only given '*lechem oni*', poor man's bread to eat. Thus, we see the 'hospitality' which the *Mitzriyim* had demonstrated towards us. With that being the case, we are meant to take this as a lesson with which we may apply to ourselves. Thus, we should say that we would never want to fall to the level of acting in that same manner of how the *Mitzriyim* treated us. The way in which we can avoid acting with such callousness, is by striving to display even **greater** care towards others. Indeed, it is for this reason that our reaction should be to call out, "כל דכפין ייתי וייכול", "all those in need may come and eat".

Chazal brought this lesson at the outset of the *Haggadah* to teach us an important principle which should be employed throughout the *seder*. The *seder* is not just about sitting back and taking a look at how we were oppressed in *Mitzrayim*. We are not meant to view the story of the *seder* like we are merely watching the story of *Mitzrayim* on a screen before us. Rather, it is important that at the beginning of the *seder* we gain the understanding that we are here to look inwardly at ourselves. The injustices that the *Mitzriyim* had brought upon us, may be used as a means of growth within ourselves, as we find ways to avoid any connection to this same type of destructive behavior. Conversely, we may show a strong desire to follow in the ways of our *heilige* ancestors from that generation who were unrelenting in their loyalty to Hashem, as they did not change their names, language or clothing.

Thus, this is the lesson that we are taught at the beginning of the *seder* in order that we view the entire *sipur yetzias Mitzrayim* "*כאילו הוא יצא ממצרים*" -- as a Divine reflection upon ourselves. This lesson is integral to us, so as to ensure that we will utilize this night as a sincere means of inner growth.

Ge'ula from the Internal and External Yetzer Horah

עבדים היינו לפרעה במצרים

After the ben is *sho'el* the '*Ma Nishtana*', we begin by answering him, "*Avadim ha'yinu le'Pharoh be'Mitzrayim...*". The Question may be raised, why was it necessary to mention that we were slaves to *Pharoh*, as well as stating that we were *avadim* in *Mitzrayim*? Would it not have been enough to merely state, "*Avadim hayinu lePharoh*"? Alternatively, it could have said, "We were slaves in *Mitzrayim*". Isn't it redundant to mention both *Pharoh* and *Mitzrayim*?

We may answer this, based upon the *Tefillah* of Rav Alexandri, which he davened upon ending *Shemone Esrei* (Berachos 17a). He stated that there are two aspects of the *Yetzer Horah* which prevent us from completing the Will of Hashem. The first, is the *se'or sheba'isa*, which refers to the Evil Inclination that is **within** the person, such as his desires and inner drives for sinfulness. Then there is the *shibud malchios* -- how the *umos ha'olam* dominate over us. Rav Alexandri would beseech Hashem, asking Him to remove from us these two facets of the *Yetzer Horah*, so that we may serve Him *be'Shleimus*.[13]

---

[13] ברכות יז עמוד א: ורבי אלכסנדרי בתר דמצלי אמר הכי: רבון העולמים, גלוי וידוע לפניך שרצוננו לעשות רצונך, ומי מעכב? שאור שבעיסה ושעבוד מלכיות; יהי רצון מלפניך שתצילנו מידם, ונשוב לעשות חוקי רצונך בלבב שלם.

The Rambam[14], refers to the *Yetzer Horah* as *Pharoh*. Thus, we can say, the name '*Pharoh*' mentioned here refers to the inner inclination, while '*Mitzrayim*' refers to the *shibud malchios*. Therefore, it may be explained, that we are thanking Hashem in this part of the *Haggadah*, for that which He had completely taken us away from the bondage of **all** divisions of the *Yetzer Horah*, both from within ourselves and from without.

One might continue to ask, we are still under the influence of the *Yetzer Horah* and *shibud malchios* today, albeit different ones than in the past. If so, for what in particular are we thanking Hashem in this part of the *haggaddah*? We may answer this in one of two ways. Firstly, it is worthwhile to recognize that every generation has its own set of desires and tendencies, as well as different impositions from each *golus* which we encounter. Thus, *Chazal* are impressing upon us, to be thankful for the situation in which Hashem has **currently** placed us. Hashem would not put us into an environment which we would not be able to withstand. Therefore, while we may look at the current situation as difficult, we can look back however, at the generation of Mitzrayim with a sense of respite, joyful that we did not need to go through their spiritual *nisyonos*.

Another difference is, that they had not yet accepted the *Torah* while they were still in Mitzrayim. Therefore, they did not yet have the ultimate means of being able to deal with the evil inclination. Now, that we do have the *Torah* with which to guide us, we are not merely given the means with

---

[14] In his letter to his son, Rav Avraham. Rav Avigdor Miller would often say this over.

which to combat the *Yetzer Horah*. Rather, through the Torah, we are able to learn how to **utilize** the *Yetzer Horah* for our benefit. For example, instead of one eating with a goal to satiate his desires, he might now learn that the *Torah* still wants him to eat with an appetite, enjoying every bite. However, it will be with a different end-purpose -- that of appreciating all that Hashem confers upon him! Indeed, the *Torah* teaches us of how to live while utilizing all of our endowments, **including** the *Yetzer Horah*.

'Hein Am Le'vadad'

והיא שעמדה לאבותינו ולנו, שלא אחד בלבד עמד עלינו לכלותינו, אלא שבכל דור ודור עומדים עלינו לכלותינו, והקב"ה מצילנו מידם.

When we read the words of "*Ve'hi she'amda*" we must ask ourselves, what is the specific *chesed* that is mentioned here of which we are thankful to Hashem? Upon first glance, we would likely all agree, that although the *umos ha'olam* have oppressed us throughout every generation, Hashem has always come to our protection and saved us from their hands.

However, upon further contemplation, we might explain this paragraph in the following manner.[15] Rav Avigdor Miller *zt"l* would often speak of the importance of *Klal Yisroel* staying separate from the world. Thus, living together in crammed 'ghettos' had its advantageous place amongst us. For, we kept together, living regal lives of *ovdei Hashem*, away from the lifestyles of the *goyim*.

Similarly, the way in which the *umos ha'olam* act towards us, also creates a vast distance between them and us.

---

[15] One may wonder that the wording of this paragraph might seem out of order. Since, it should first state the problem: "*Lo echad bilvad amad aleinu le'chaloseinu, ela she'bichol dor va'dor omdim aleinu le'chaloseinu*". Only **after** stating the subjugation of the *goyim* upon us, would it be the right place to declare, "*Ve'hi sh'amda la'avoseinu ve'lanu...*", and **this** is what stood for us and our fathers -- that Hashem had always protected us from them.

Imagine walking down the city street, says Rav Miller, and suddenly you hear the drunken bum who is in the gutter, call out to you. "Filthy Jew", he screams out from amongst the refuse in which he is lying. Your reaction to him should be nothing less than a tremendous feeling of joy! You should cry out to Hashem, "Thank You, for this reminder to keep separate from them!". Hashem wants us to live elevated, royal lives as His servants. However, this can only be accomplished through our segregation from the goyim. Therefore, He helps us achieve our purpose in life, through the built-in enmity which they feel towards us.

Returning to the above paragraph, we may now understand that the chesed Hashem which we mention here, is not only that Hashem brings us yeshu'os from the goyim. Rather, we are thankful to Hashem in this part of the *Haggadah*, on two accounts. "...והיא שעמדה לאבותינו ולנו" **This** is what stood for us throughout all generations. Firstly, שלא אחד בלבד" "עמד עלינו לכלותינו, אלא שבכל דור ודור עומדים עלינו לכלותינו. We are grateful to Hashem that He had devised a masterplan of keeping us separate and above the ways of the *goyim*, through their hostility towards us. However, this is not all. For, after we remain distinct from them, He does not forsake us. "והקב"ה מצילנו מידם" -- Hashem protects us from their hands.

Pesach, Matzah and Maror

כָּל שֶׁלֹּא אָמַר שְׁלשָׁה דְּבָרִים אֵלּוּ בַּפֶּסַח לֹא יָצָא יְדֵי חוֹבָתוֹ וְאֵלּוּ הֵן, פֶּסַח מַצָּה וּמָרוֹר

In the Haggadah Shel Pesach, as we reach the end of *Maggid*, Rabban Gamliel makes an important statement:[16]

כָּל שֶׁלֹּא אָמַר שְׁלשָׁה דְּבָרִים אֵלּוּ בַּפֶּסַח לֹא יָצָא יְדֵי חוֹבָתוֹ וְאֵלּוּ הֵן, פֶּסַח מַצָּה וּמָרוֹר -

Anyone who does not say these three things on Pesach has not fulfilled his obligation. They are: (Korban) Pesach, matzah, and maror.

These three things are integral to understanding the *ge'ulas Mitzrayim* (Redemption from Egypt). The *Pesach* signifies that Hashem passed over the Jewish homes on the night of *Makkas Bechoros*. *Matzah* shows that the Bnei Yisroel left Mitzrayim so hurriedly that they did not even have time to allow their dough rise before they left. The *maror* was also an integral part of the *ge'ulah*, for it shows how the Mitzriyim embittered our lives in Mitzrayim. Mitzrayim was the *kur ha'barzel* (the iron kiln) for Bnei Yisroel, which means that it refined us throughout our stay there. Thus, the embittered life we experienced was an important part of *galus* and *ge'ulas Mitzrayim*.

---

[16] Originally found in a Mishnah in Maseches Pesachim, 116b.

However, we may ask why Rabban Gamliel presents these three things in this specific order? We understand that *Pesach* precedes *matzah*, for this is the chronological order in which they occurred. But *maror* - the embittered life that the Jews lived in Mitzrayim - took place **before** *Pesach* and *matzah*. If so, why is it mentioned last?

Perhaps we can answer that, yes, the *merirus* – bitterness - took place before the actual *ge'ulah*. However, the importance of the difficulties was first **made clear** to the Jews after the *ge'ulah* itself. As we mentioned above, the embitterment that they experienced was a very necessary part of their growth. However, when one is going through adversity, it is most difficult to see the 'good' that may come from it. One who is in the midst of suffering is not ready to hear about the 'goodness' that is inherent in his difficulties. It is only after one reaches the light at the end of the tunnel; once one actually experiences the freedom from bondage, that he is able to look back and focus on the light during the darkness. It is then that he can happily say that even the difficult times were part and parcel of his growth throughout his ordeal.

Thus, Rabban Gamliel is not merely teaching us the three primary points of the *ge'ulas Mitzrayim*. Rather, he is also teaching us that the embitterment was integral to *ge'ulas Mitzrayim*, the exodus from Egypt. Only, we couldn't possibly see what was being accomplished while we were living through it. Only after *Pesach* and *matzah* - after the actual *ge'ulah* – were we able to understand the important place of *maror* in this chain of events.

Acharon shel Pesach
Perfection of The Mind: Conquering the Enemy from Within

On *Acharon shel Pesach* (the seventh day of Pesach) we say only half Hallel, unlike the first days of Pesach, when we say the complete Hallel. The Beis Yosef (490:4) quotes the Medrash, also found in the Yalkut Shimoni (Emor, 654), that the reason we do not say a full Hallel on the seventh day is because the Mitzriyim drowned then. Chazal apply the *posuk* in Mishlei (24:17), which states explicitly:

- בִּנְפֹל אוֹיִבְךָ אַל־תִּשְׂמָח וּבִכָּשְׁלוֹ אַל־יָגֵל לִבֶּךָ

Do not rejoice at the downfall of your enemy, and when he stumbles, your heart should not regale.[17]

This Medrash presents a problem. After all, we see that Bnei Yisroel sang *shirah* at length at the *Yam Suf*, clearly indicating that they openly rejoiced at the downfall of their enemies. They did not curtail their *simchah* or the *shirah* for the sake of not rejoicing at the downfall of their enemy!

---

[17] On Chol Hamoed, we also say only half-Hallel, so that the intermediate days should not be greater than the last day, which is Yom Tov itself.

Moreover, Chazal tell us that Bnei Yisroel **may** show *simchah* at the downfall of their foes (Megillah 10b). In fact, there are a number of *pesukim* that state openly that one may experience joy at the downfall of the wicked. For example, in Mishlei (11:10) it says:

- וּבַאֲבֹד רְשָׁעִים רִנָּה

with the loss of the wicked comes joy.

How do we reconcile this dichotomy?

It can possibly be explained based on the following statement from Pirkei Avos (4:23), in which Shmuel Hakatan teaches, 'בִּנְפֹל אוֹיִבְךָ אַל־תִּשְׂמָח וכו – *do not rejoice at the downfall of your enemy...*

The obvious question posed by the *meforshim* is what novel idea did *Shmuel Hakatan* teach us? He merely repeats a posuk, which we've quoted above.

Perhaps we can answer this question with an insight from the *Medrash Shmuel* on how to deal with one's enemies. The Medrash Shmuel explains, based on a posuk,[18] that the way of a truly humble person is to try to find peace within himself not only when dealing with Hashem, but even when dealing with his enemies. This, he explains, was the *middah* of Shmuel Hakatan himself, who the gemara tells us was

---

[18] בִּרְצוֹת ה' דַּרְכֵי־אִישׁ גַּם־אוֹיְבָיו יַשְׁלִם אִתּוֹ – *When Hashem is satisfied with the ways of man, his enemies will make peace with him too* (Mishlei 16:7).

called "the small one" because he was exceedingly humble. His humility afforded him the ability not just to act in a humble manner before Hashem, but also in his conduct with his enemies. By contrast, the one who is joyous at his enemy's demise may feel an overpowering feeling of arrogance.

We may now answer that this saying that was said by Shmuel Hakatan does not, in fact, teach us anything new in itself, for it is an explicit *posuk*, as we said above. The *chiddush* is in **who** said it. Shmuel Hakatan is teaching us that it is essential for a Jew to acquire a proper *shleimus* in his *dei'os* (mindset). Therefore, yes, it's true that there is a reason for one to excessively rejoice when his enemy who is a *rasha* falls. But that is specifically when the person is on the level of *emunah* at which there is **no question** that his feelings are stemming from service of Hashem. Only then can one be confident that he will be acquiring the *shleimus hada'as* (completeness of mind) for the sake of Heaven as a result of seeing the downfall of the enemies of Hashem, and not because of his own feelings of superiority.

However, for most of us, we must worry that our *middah* of haughtiness will likely overtake us when we rejoice over our enemies' downfall. Therefore, it is **specifically** Shmuel Hakatan, the great *Anav*, who says how he lived by this posuk - **not** to be overly joyous at their loss. We must learn from him to inculcate a *shleimus* of the *middah* of *anavah* in our minds so as not to arrogantly rejoice over the downfall of our enemies.

Conversely, Bnei Yisroel at the Yam Suf had reached the highest levels of *emunah*. Their sincerity in acquiring a true *shleimus hada'as* was beyond anything we can fathom. Therefore, **for them, on their level**, the proper approach to *shleimus hada'as* was to excessively rejoice at the downfall of their enemies. Doing so meant gaining a greater *emunah* in the *schar v'onesh* (reward and punishment) of Hashem - to see His heavenly retribution against His true foes.[19]

---

[19] In actuality, there are two schools of thought as to the correct approach towards the downfall of one's enemies. According to Rav Avigdor Miller, it is the job of man to shower uninhibited praise upon Hashem for the loss of *reshaim*. This results in a greater perfection of one's *da'as*. (See Praise My Soul, paragraph 414.) On the other hand, there are great *ba'alei mussar* who felt, as we stated above, that the enmity expressed towards one's enemies often stems from a feeling of *ga'avah* over them, an abhorrent *middah* which one must eradicate from within himself. This may be demonstrated through the following anecdote. There was a *bochur* in the Slabodka Yeshiva who took upon himself the stringency to begin *Shabbos* considerably earlier than the proper time. When the Alter found out about this, he confronted this *talmid* and asked him, "Tell me - you already accepted *Shabbos* upon yourself, and your friends are still doing weekday activity, since, after all, there is still plenty of time until *Shabbos*. How do you look upon your friends during this time? Indeed, you look upon them as though they are transgressing *Shabbos*! If so, it's worthwhile for you to drop this *chumrah*, and do as everyone else. The main thing to be careful about is to not look down on others who don't keep your stringencies" (Shiurei Chumash, Shemos, 23:5). Similarly, explains Rav Shlomo Wolbe, this is how one feels when seeing an enemy fall. Unless one is of a very exalted stature, he will undoubtedly feel pride over the fact that he is in a greater position than his enemy. That thought alone is enough to counter the benefit of effusively praising Hashem over the downfall of one's enemies.

Made in United States
North Haven, CT
16 February 2022